IT'S US.

How Can I Sort out the Issues of my family Life?

Participant's Guide

A Reel to Real Study

Nicole Johnson
Mary E. Demuth

THOMAS NELSON
Since 1798

NASHVILLE   DALLAS   MEXICO CITY   RIO DE JANEIRO

D1445298

Published in Nashville, Tennessee, by Thomas Nelson. Thomas Nelson is a registered trademark of Thomas Nelson, Inc.

Thomas Nelson, Inc., titles may be purchased in bulk for educational, business, fund-raising, or sales promotional use. For information, please e-mail SpecialMarkets@thomasnelson.com.

ISBN: 978-1-4185-4639-7

Reel to Real: An Interactive Drama-Based Study Series

It's Us: How Can I Sort Out the Issues of My Family Life?

Printed in the United States of America

11 12 13 14 15 QG 5 4 3 2 1

contents:

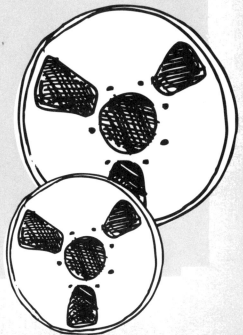

What Is a Reel to Real Study?

Simply put, it's what you hold in your hands. A video sketch (reel) and your journey (real). Put those two together and you have a fresh and transforming way of studying the Bible and getting to know God.

We are so excited you've decided to journey alongside us in this adventure called following Jesus. Knowing the current bent toward YouTube, iTunes, and social networking sites, we've developed an interactive study based on that reality. You'll watch a drama, hear from others who are on the journey, and then chat about it with your friends. We've provided many different ways for you to grow.

The sketches you'll see on the DVD are dramatic vignettes written and directed by Nicole Johnson. Each drama was performed and recorded live at the Revolve Tour and put together for this study as a creative way to look at the issues we face.

This guide will be your companion as you watch the dramas. The first study is designed for group interaction. Of course, you can always watch the DVD on your own and work your way through the study if you'd like. But we find gathering a group of friends to watch the drama, then discussing it together over popcorn and caffeine makes the learning fun. More people equal more discussion, more insight.

After the initial watch and discuss, we offer four more studies for you to explore each theme on your own. Like taking a walk in your own woods, you can go as deep as you dare and stay as long as you wish, hopefully emerging at some point with a clearer understanding of how you can live differently in this changing world.

These personal studies will not be your typical Bible study where you take a crusty ballpoint and fill in long blanks with short answers. We'll ask you probing questions that definitely don't have a set answer. You'll tap into your creativity. We'll push you (gently!) toward thinking about the world outside your front door. We'll start you with a truth, but you'll end with a dare. Then we'll resource you with cool sites, books, and songs that can help you further your journey.

It's our hope that by watching this DVD, digesting it with friends, and doing some thinking and wrestling on your own, you'll finish the study a little different from how you were when you started. More confident of who you are. More able to open your heart to who God is and willing to be surprised by His extravagant, countercultural love. Released to be who He created you to be. And full of gratitude for all He has done (and will continue do) inside you and through you.

The world needs your heart. Your real heart. Not some phony replica of what you think your heart should look like—a real, unique heart. Our desire is to see that heart challenged, shaped, and doing revolutions around Jesus, as He revolves around this world.

- Nicole and Mary

P.S. For more information about the Revolve Tour or just to see what this dynamic conference is all about, check out **www.revolvetour.com**.

IT'S US. Introduction:

We all have families. Some are big. Some are small. We're all connected in some way to relatives young and old, parents who share life with us. Maybe we have sisters and brothers. Maybe one parent, maybe two. Sometimes we argue. Misunderstand one another. Other times, we experience the comfortable joy of just being together.

God's initial plan way back in the garden of Eden was to give us a place to belong, struggle, share, and bear burdens. So He created families. Of all the things He created, including his masterpiece, Adam, God said, "It is good." But when the first man God created felt utterly alone in the garden, "Then the Lord God said, 'It is not good for the man to be alone. I will make a helper who is right for him'" (Genesis 2:18, NCV).

It wasn't good for Adam to be alone. He needed and wanted someone to share his life and heart with. So God gave him a wife, Eve, and from Adam and Eve came the first family. And from then on everything was perfect, right?

Wrong.

From the moment sin entered the garden, strife roared to life. The first family struggled. A hatred-filled rivalry grew between brothers Cain and Abel, ending with Cain murdering his brother, then lying about it. Clearly, things weren't all roses and cupcakes, even in the midst of what God Himself had designed.

> *It wasn't good for Adam to be alone. He needed and wanted someone to share his life and heart with.*

Aside from the murder part, we've all experienced angry thoughts when it comes to family. It's the people we love the most who have the greatest potential to hurt us. And yet, it's those very people God uses to keep us feeling loved and stable. Seems odd, doesn't it?

And yet we know from Scripture that God places us where we are, right smack-dab in the middle of our families. Don't believe it? Read this: "God places the lonely in families; he sets the prisoners free and gives them joy. But he makes the rebellious live in a sun-scorched land" (Psalm 68:6, NLT).

The last part of this verse seems to foreshadow the New Testament story of the prodigal son. This young man wanted life outside the circle of his God-given family members more than he wanted their protection. So the prodigal son ventured, wandered, and then squandered everything he owned. He lived in self-imposed exile in that "sun-scorched land," broke, starving, and hankering after pig slop. When he finally came to his senses, he walked home, head down in shame. He expected a thrashing, but instead received the wide-open arms of his father. (See Luke 15:11–32 for the whole story.)

Like the prodigal son, some of you may have experienced deep and amazing grace from your parents. Some of you may feel rejection from those you love the most. But the great news is that, for those who follow Jesus, we get a new family. We get to know a Father—God—who welcomes us with wide-open arms. Even when our families fail to meet our expectations, even when they frustrate or wound us, God is always waiting on tiptoes at the top of a dusty hill, straining to see us, if we decide to walk home. He opens wide His arms, gathers Himself up to run, and welcomes us again and again into His family, His acceptance, and His love.

As you work your way through these studies, remember this part of God—His fatherly desire to be in a good relationship with you, and to see you whole and healed and restored by His love. Try to remember that no family is perfect. We all have our warts and quirks. But God has strategically placed you just where you are to learn to love people—some you like, and some you don't like so much, but just like all of us, with faults and needs aplenty.

they drive me crazy

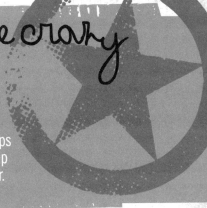

BRIEF OUTTAKE: A girl, a guy, a mom, and a dad—and a teacher—discuss and complain about one another. Interestingly, they all seem to have the same beef—lots of misunderstandings and frustration. But perhaps seeing things from another perspective will help them learn to respect one another a little better.

 watch dvd episode 1.

GROUP STUDY:

 Truth. ←——————————————

Go around your circle and share the answer to these questions (and remember to tell the truth!):

Q: If you have conflicts with your parents, whose fault is it most of the time in terms of percentages? (40 percent you, 60 percent them?)

Q: What one thing do you love about your family right now?

Q: What are the things that drive you crazy about your parents?

9

Read Jake's Story:

My father was my hero. I remember following him around like he owned the world. I really thought he did. He always took time for me, especially for a game of catch in the lot next door. I can still see him laughing and crouching low to catch my wobbly throws.

But then he got a promotion. He was gone from home a lot traveling. Mom grew kinda distant, and not much fun to be with. One night I heard her tell Grandma that she felt abandoned. I know I did. Dad never came home before I went to bed. I'd stay up as late as Mom would let me, just hoping I'd get to see him, but most of the time I'd wake up in the morning and he'd already be gone . . . again.

> **My father was my hero. I remember following him around like he owned the world. I really thought he did.**

Once I woke up in the night because I heard them yelling. Mom was crying. I cracked my door and saw Dad standing in the kitchen. He said to Mom in a voice I hardly recognized, "I never loved you." I felt a weight press down on my chest and I couldn't breathe.

"Is there someone else?"

When Dad said yes, I thought I was gonna hurl. Or cry, if I knew how. Instead, I slammed my door and punched it as hard as I could and just kept kicking and kicking it. One knuckle and two fingers on my hand were broken, but I didn't know it at the time, or care.

I told my dad I hated him. That he wasn't my hero or anybody's.

He moved out. It lasted eight months with his girlfriend. Only then did he call me up, wanting to "make amends" as he said. I didn't want anything to do with him. Still don't.

He says I don't understand him. I don't. How can you understand someone you don't know?

I'll admit this: I hurt so bad. I miss playing catch. I miss having a dad.

Q: **Have you or a friend of yours ever experienced any events like Jake experienced? What happened?**

Q: **Do you feel your issues at home have more to do with misunderstanding one another or simply not knowing one another? Why or why not?**

Word. ←————————————————————

What does the Bible say about our relationships with our family?

read:

For where two or three are gathered together in My name, I am there in the midst of them.
(Matthew 18:20, NKJV)

This verse applies to the family too.

Q: Is it strange to think when you're gathered with your family that God is in your midst? Why or why not? Is laughing holy?

Is not wisdom found among the aged? Does not long life bring understanding?
(Job 12:12, NIV)

Q: Give one piece of advice you've received from your parents or grandparents that has proved to be helpful and true.

Children, obey your parents in the Lord, for this is right. "Honor your father and mother"—which is the first commandment with a promise—"that it may go well with you and that you may enjoy long life on the earth."

Fathers, do not exasperate your children; instead, bring them up in the training and instruction of the Lord.
(Ephesians 6:1–4, NIV)

Q: What do you think it means to honor your parents? How have you honored your parents this week?

Q: In what ways have you dishonored them?

Q: What do you think this means: "Fathers, do not exasperate your children"? Have your parents ever exasperated you? When? Were you able to share your frustration with them? Did they listen to you?

> *Children, obey your parents in the Lord, for this is right.*
> EPHESIANS 6:1, NIV

Q: If you have children one day, what would it look like to train them in the "instruction of the Lord"?

Q: What have your parents done well in training you to love Jesus? What do you wish they would've done differently?

My dear brothers, take note of this: Everyone should be quick to listen, slow to speak and slow to become angry, for man's anger does not bring about the righteous life that God desires.

(James 1:19–20, NIV)

Q: When have you been slow to listen to your parents?

Q: What is the danger of being quick to speak?

Q: How about being quick to become angry?

Q: How have your parents been slow to listen, quick to speak?

Q: Why doesn't our anger bring about the kind of life God wants?

Q: What does anger look like in your home? What does harmony look like?

Get rid of all bitterness, rage and anger, brawling and slander, along with every form of malice. Be kind and compassionate to one another, forgiving each other, just as in Christ God forgave you.

(Ephesians 4:31–32, NIV)

Q: When was the last time you apologized to your parents?

Q: How have your parents asked you for forgiveness?

Q: Recall a time when you admitted you did something wrong to your parents. What happened? What kind of impression did that leave on you?

Q: Who in your family (in either your close or extended family) lives a life of bitterness? Why does he/she live that way, in your opinion?

Q: If someone observed the way you treated your family, would they say you are usually kind and compassionate?

Talk.

Activity: Role-play.

In the drama, the kids and parents had the same frustrations with one another. These kinds of frustrations are pretty common among parents and kids. In your group, brainstorm a situation that causes frustration and then act out that situation, giving each person a role to play (mom, dad, child, sibling, etc.) and a positive or negative ending. Here are the five frustrations:

1. They don't listen to us.
2. They don't understand anything.
3. They contradict themselves all the time.
4. The only word they know is *no*.
5. They are always correcting us.

Q: What surprised you about your role-playing activity?

Q: For those playing parents, was it easy to step into those shoes? Why or why not?

So what does all this have to do with you?

Q: When was the last time you felt ignored by your parents or brothers and sisters?

Q: What one thing do you wish your parents would understand about you? Have you ever tried to communicate this to them?

Q: Do you think there is anything your parents wish you could understand about them? Would you consider asking them?

Q: In the drama, each could point out the contradictions of the other. How do you contradict yourself? How do your parents contradict themselves?

Q: In what kinds of situations do your parents say no? Are there times when you agree with their no even if you don't like it?

When was the last time you felt ignored by your parents or brothers and sisters?

Q: How do you correct your parents?

Sometimes we fight about the same things over and over with our parents. It feels like we're just reading from the same script as last time and nothing gets accomplished except louder yelling.

Q: What is your most common fight with your parents? What do you say? What do they repeat?

★ Activity: Say What?

Toward the end of the drama, you hear lots of parentisms and teenisms—things parents and teens commonly say to one another. Here are some examples:

- Stand up straight.
- Don't lecture me.
- Don't chew with your mouth open.
- Don't touch my stuff.

Divide into two groups. One group has to come up with common teenisms, the other listing common parentisms. You have two minutes. At the end, compare lists and see which team comes up with the most.

Some parentisms are funny, like, "If you poke your eye out, don't come crying to me!" And did you ever think about the fact that you can't poke your eye out? Really. You can only poke it in.

Q: Which parentism drives you the craziest?

Okay, be honest. Some teenisms are pretty ridiculous too. Like, "Everyone is going!" Really? Everyone? Hmmm.

Q: Which teenism could be dropped from your vocabulary? What kind of reaction do you get when you say it?

Pray. ←

Activity: Left and right.

Supplies needed:
- Individual notebook papers
- Pens

Fold a piece of lined notebook paper in half vertically. On the left side, write the words *Right Now*. On the right side, write, *What I'd Like It to Be*.

On the left-hand side of your paper, list how your family is doing right now. The highs and lows, frustrations and joys, understandings and misunderstandings. You don't need to share this with anyone.

On the right-hand side of the paper, write what you'd like to see changed about your family. Ways that you wish it could be.

Now fold the paper and place it somewhere safe. Commit to pray for your family about these things, present and future, this week. Ask God to show you one thing you can do, or one way He could use you to bring about one of these changes.

For praying together in this group, choose one thing from your list, either past or future, and share it with a partner. Then listen to your partner's one thing. Together, pray about the other's concern.

> **Commit to pray for your family about these things, present and future, this week.**

create.

ACTIVITY: The family table.

A bowl of vegetables with someone you love is better than steak with someone you hate.
(Proverbs 15:17, NLT)

Supplies needed:
- One sheet of plain white paper
- Scissors, glue stick, colored pens or pencils
- Magazines

On a blank sheet of paper, draw your dinner table. If you don't eat together as a family, draw a place where you gather with your family—outside, on the couch, in front of the TV. Then draw a place for each person, something like this:

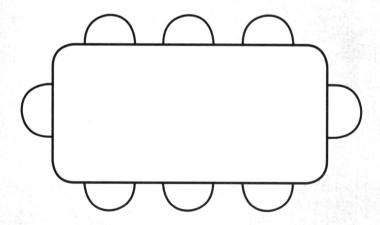

Cut out pictures that represent each person and paste each in his/her chair. (This isn't necessary, but it might be fun.)

Now it's time to color.

1. Draw a straight green line between you and the people in your family you can talk to without it becoming stressful.
2. Draw a black crisscross line between you and someone you have a hard time talking to.
3. Draw a blue wavy line between you and someone who has hurt you recently.
4. Draw a broken red line between you and someone you're currently angry with.
5. Draw a yellow line between you and someone who brings you joy.
6. Now using all the same types of lines, draw them between each family member. (For instance, if your sister and brother get along really well, draw a straight green line between them. If your father and your oldest brother have yelled at each other recently, draw a red broken line between them.)

Take a look at your drawing. What color dominates? What color doesn't show up much? What relationship would you like to see change for the better?

read:

"In your anger do not sin": Do not let the sun go down while you are still angry, and do not give the devil a foothold.

(Ephesians 4:26–27, NIV)

Q: How can you be angry, but not sin? In Jake's story, earlier in this study, he was angry. Do you think he sinned? What does it look like for the devil to have a foothold in your life? How does anger invite his activity in your life?

He who conceals his sins does not prosper, but whoever confesses and renounces them finds mercy.

(Proverbs 28:13, NIV)

Q: Of the people around your table, who conceals (or hides) sins? Do you? Why or why not?

Keep this drawing and use it as a prayer picture. Ask God to change or heal the relationships around your table. Pray that He will bring restoration when there has been anger or misunderstanding.

"In your anger do not sin": Do not let the sun go down while you are still angry, and do not give the devil a foothold.
EPHESIANS 4:26–27, NIV

When praying for the broken relationships in your family, don't view them as "their" problems. Ask God to make you a part of the solution by showing you things you can do. Stuff like:

1. Dear Lord, help me to be slow to anger when it comes to my dad. He really knows how to press my buttons.
2. I need more patience with my brother's bossiness.
3. I've been angry with my mom a long time. Today I choose, by Your strength, to begin to forgive her.
4. Forgive me for choosing to misunderstand my sister rather than sitting down and really listening to her. Help me to be slow to jump to conclusions.
5. Give me a desire to truly connect with my family.

deep.

I want my own way. I want to be understood.

A lot of our issues with our parents or family members boil down to selfishness on all sides. We demand to be understood and heard, but we don't offer the same kindness to our families. Isn't it sad that most people treat perfect strangers better than they do the people who live within the four walls of their homes?

A home is supposed to be a haven. What is a haven? It's a place of refuge. A safe place. A sanctuary from the craziness of life.

One reason why a home may not be a haven stems from the family members only thinking about themselves.

The author of the book of James agrees.

read:

> *Isn't it sad that most people treat perfect strangers better than they do the people who live within the four walls of their homes?*

What causes fights and quarrels among you? Don't they come from your desires that battle within you? You want something but don't get it. You kill and covet, but you cannot have what you want. You quarrel and fight. You do not have, because you do not ask God. When you ask, you do not receive, because you ask with wrong motives, that you may spend what you get on your pleasures.

(James 4:1–3, NIV)

You might be saying, "Yeah, I wish my mom would read that verse and start applying it." Yes, and hopefully she will, but the deeper truth? You can't change your mom's behavior, or anyone else's for that matter. You can pray for your family and hope they change, but the only thing you can change is you. You are a vital part of your family. You are a piece of the haven pie. A home can only be as safe as its least safe member.

Think about this: When was the last time you asked God to help you love your family?

Q: What was the last fight you had with your parents? How did that fight result from "desires that battle within you"?

Think through how the fight might've changed had everyone chosen selflessness instead of selfishness.

read:

We who are strong must be considerate of those who are sensitive about things like this. We must not just please ourselves. We should help others do what is right and build them up in the Lord. For even Christ didn't live to please himself. As the Scriptures say, "The insults of those who insult you, O God, have fallen on me." Such things were written in the Scriptures long ago to teach us. And the Scriptures give us hope and encouragement as we wait patiently for God's promises to be fulfilled.

May God, who gives this patience and encouragement, help you live in complete harmony with each other, as is fitting for followers of Christ Jesus. Then all of you can join together with one voice, giving praise and glory to God, the Father of our Lord Jesus Christ.

Therefore, accept each other just as Christ has accepted you so that God will be given glory.
(Romans 15:1–7, NLT)

Q: **What would it look like to build up your parents in the Lord?**

Q: **What would it look like in your home to have complete harmony, or at least more than there is now?**

Q: **How well do you accept your parents? How well do they accept you? Is it possible you are both waiting on each other for the acceptance you both long for?**

Q: **When was the last time you felt your family joined "together with one voice, giving praise and glory to God"? What happened?**

Q: **What does it mean to accept your family members? Does acceptance mean agreement? What's the difference, if there is one? And why do you think accepting others in your family makes God smile (gives Him glory)?**

pray:

Lord, I want there to be harmony in my home. I want to help create a haven. Show me how to let go of myself more often, thinking first of the needs of my family. Help me to love and forgive in ways that honor You. Give me strength to not sin if I feel angry, but instead to trust You with it. By Your power, bring even more joy into my family through me. I trust You. Amen.

The Gratitude Attitude

BY TODD M. CLEMENTS, M.D.

It's easy (and almost second nature) to look at the lives of people around you and start feeling discontent with your own life. Teenage girls often do this when they start thinking things like:

- *I wish I had hair like Susan's.*
- *I wish my parents were more like Kristen's.*
- *Why can't I be as smart as Jackie? She seems to have it all.*

Did you know that feeling discontentment has negative effects on both your physical and mental health? It's true. Discontented people experience more feelings of anxiety, irritability, anger, and sadness.

A large research study showed that people who wrote down five things that they were grateful for each day and then spent two minutes thinking about each item felt better overall than another group, who spent the same ten minutes each day thinking about five things that irritated them.

The grateful group reported both physical and mental benefits after only three weeks. They felt more relaxed and calm and had more energy throughout the day. They also felt their contentment level rise in their daily lives—when nothing had changed but their attitude.

Do you find yourself ever feeling discontent with your life? Then I challenge you to take ten minutes out of each day to write down and focus on five things you are grateful for. If you'll do this for a whole month you'll be surprised by the results of your "Gratitude Attitude." And your friends and family may be pleasantly surprised too.

After all, it's what the Bible instructs us to do. In 1st Thessalonians 5:18 (NIV) the apostle Paul encourages us to "give thanks in all circumstances." Gratitude is simply the best way to ensure there is no "dis" in our content.

Dr. Todd Clements *is a board-certified psychiatrist and is the medical director of the Clements Clinic in Plano, Texas.*

wide.

Rules rule.

Chances are your relationship with your parents has changed over time. You may have felt distant from them in grade school, but found a way to draw closer in junior high. Or the opposite happened. This is not only common, but normal. Relationships change. A lot.

But one thing that doesn't change is that parents are called to walk alongside their children and help them grow in their understanding of God.

Read about this role:

Hear, O Israel: The Lord our God, the Lord is one. Love the Lord your God with all your heart and with all your soul and with all your strength. These commandments that I give you today are to be upon your hearts. Impress them on your children. Talk about them when you sit at home and when you walk along the road, when you lie down and when you get up. Tie them as symbols on your hands and bind them on your foreheads. Write them on the doorframes of your houses and on your gates.

Relationships change. A lot.

(Deuteronomy 6:4–9, NIV)

Q: How have your parents impressed these truths upon you? How do you talk about Jesus at home? Or have you ever?

This passage seems to say that children learn as they spend time together with their parents.

Q: Are you satisfied with how much time you spend with your parents? What would you change about how often you talk with them?

Q: According to this passage, what are parents to teach their children?

Q: Many Jewish families still write God's truths on their doorframes. For Christians, what does it look like to love God with all your heart, soul, and mind in your home?

A refusal to correct is a refusal to love; love your children by disciplining them.
(Proverbs 13:24, MSG)

Q: Are there any ways that you are thankful for your parents' rules? Which ones in particular?

Q: Rules change over time ("You can't cross the street without holding my hand"), gradually moving toward more freedom ("Be home by midnight"). How have your rules changed, fairly or unfairly, over the past three years?

List your rules, if you have any, in the following areas:

1. Curfew
2. How you spend your free time
3. Money
4. Computer use
5. Video game time
6. Cell phone/texting
7. Friendships
8. Homework
9. Chores
10. Dating

> *Rules change over time ("You can't cross the street without holding my hand"), gradually moving toward more freedom ("Be home by midnight").*

Q: What would you say is the overarching "rule" or way in your home? Here are some possibilities:

1. Listen first.
2. Respect each other.
3. Others before self.
4. When in doubt, ask.
5. Don't argue back.
6. Choose forgiveness.
7. Work for the greater good of the family.
8. With greater freedom comes greater responsibility.
9. Conversation over conflict.
10. What would Jesus do?

One of the most difficult things about families is building trust. Once trust is broken, it's hard to earn it back. Think of trust like a bank—a trust fund, if you will. If you want your parents to trust you, you need to consistently make deposits by meeting their expectations. Things like:

1. Following directions the first time.
2. Keeping your room clean (or at least presentable).
3. Backing down when an argument escalates.
4. Meeting curfews early—each and every time.
5. Doing what you say you will do.
6. Following through on chores, with excellence.
7. Doing things before you're asked to do them.
8. Going out of your way to bless your parents or siblings.
9. Giving up something you want to do for the sake of a family outing.
10. Volunteering to do an unpopular chore.

On the other hand, if parents break trust, they also have to consistently demonstrate their trustworthiness before trust can be reestablished. It's their job, too, to make deposits and build into that trust fund.

What are some withdrawals you've made in the trust fund lately? What about your parents—have they made any withdrawals?

Q: In what ways are you building into your trust fund?

Q: What are some withdrawals you've made in the trust fund lately? What about your parents—have they made any withdrawals? In the story, Jake's father withdrew so much from his family. What could he do to begin to make deposits again?

Q: What would it take for you to truly trust your parents?

Q: Do you feel you are truly trustworthy? Remember, trust is earned, not granted.

read:

Dear children, let us not love with words or tongue but with actions and in truth.
(1 John 3:18, NIV)

As you know, words only mean as much as the actions that back them. Pray today that your actions will confirm your trustworthiness to your parents.

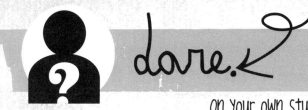

ACTiViTY: WriTe iT down.

Sometimes there are people in our lives who just do not understand us. No matter what we do, we can't change the misunderstanding. And hardest of all is when that person is a parent.

Choose one parent (or relative) who tends to misunderstand you. Now give yourself permission to write it all down in a letter to him/her—the misunderstandings, what really happened, your frustrations, your own part in the problem. Be raw. Be real. Write it all down.

Finish the letter, but don't send it. In a very real way, this represents one of the deepest prayers of your heart.

If you dare:

Pray over your letter. Pray that God would give you an opportunity to share your heart (not your letter) with your parent or family member. Remember, it's not dishonoring to share the truth, as long as it is shared from a heart of love.

Pray that God would give you an opportunity to share your heart (not your letter) with your parent or family member.

Resources & iTunes List

Resources.

- *Getting a Grip: The Heart of Anger Handbook for Teens*, by Lou Priolo
- *Nine Things Teens Should Know and Parents Are Afraid to Talk About*, by Joe White and Nicholas Comninellis
- *The Book of Questions*, by Gregory Stock, Ph.D.

 Listen. ←――――――――――――――――――

- "How to Save a Life" by The Fray, *How to Save a Life*
- "Family" by Feist, *Monarch: Lay Down Your Jewelled Head*
- "Just Between You and Me" by dc Talk, *Jesus Freak*
- "Maybe There's a Loving God" by Sara Groves, *All Right Here*
- "Daughters" by John Mayer, *Heavier Things*

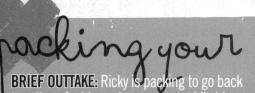

packing your stuff

BRIEF OUTTAKE: Ricky is packing to go back to college for his sophomore year while his little sister Libby packs for camp. Libby wants to do all the packing on her own, while her mom wants to help her make better choices. Ricky looks back over his freshman year and decides he wants to make better choices.

watch dvd episode 2.

Group StuDy:

Truth. ←

Go around your circle and share the answer to these questions (and remember to tell the truth!):

Q: When you last packed for camp or vacation, did your mom help you? Why or why not?

Q: What is the silliest thing you've ever packed? Were you glad you packed it?

Q: What's something you really regretted forgetting to pack?

Q: Would you ever let your parents pick out your clothes on your first day of school? Why or why not? Did they do this when you were little?

Q: How old were you when your parents stop setting out your clothes for you?

Read Shaunti's Story:

It wasn't like I needed it. I didn't. In fact, I had several tubes of lip gloss at home, tucked neatly into my makeup drawer. But another one enticed me at the store. Bubble gum pink, it said. I opened it, smelled it, thought about the money in my purse. Not enough.

So I took it.

I take things I don't need.

Why?

I wish I could answer that. It goes back to the trash bag, I guess. When the authorities took me away to the foster home, one man shoved a Hefty bag my way and told me to pack everything I needed.

> *I needed so much, but the bag was only so big. I shoved things into it until it stretched gray. I was careful to include Sally, my favorite doll. She had the most pretty pink lips.*

I needed so much, but the bag was only so big. I shoved things into it until it stretched gray. I was careful to include Sally, my favorite doll. She had the most pretty pink lips.

I could barely lug the bag to the car. And then it tore as I drug it across my gravel driveway. The officer seemed impatient with me. He grabbed the bag and threw it in the trunk. As we pulled away, I saw Sally there on the driveway, her hand reaching for me.

Now I worry I won't have enough. So I take things. Problem is, I don't want to live this way anymore. I want to be content. I don't want to want things I think I need. I want to grow up. Besides that, I know stealing is wrong and it hurts Jesus—and my foster parents. But I'm so afraid.

Q: Shaunti did her own type of packing, involving shoplifting. Have you ever been tempted to take something that wasn't yours?

Q: Have you ever overpacked for something because you were afraid of not having enough?

Q: What kind of advice would you offer Shaunti?

word.

read:

Now the Bereans were of more noble character than the Thessalonians, for they received the message with great eagerness and examined the Scriptures every day to see if what Paul said was true.

(Acts 17:11, NIV)

Q: How does reading the Bible help you understand your own faith better?

Q: In what ways have you been like a Berean, searching the Bible after you hear a new teaching?

Have nothing to do with godless myths and old wives' tales; rather, train yourself to be godly. For physical training is of some value, but godliness has value for all things, holding promise for both the present life and the life to come.

This is a trustworthy saying that deserves full acceptance (and for this we labor and strive), that we have put our hope in the living God, who is the Savior of all men, and especially of those who believe.

Command and teach these things. Don't let anyone look down on you because you are young, but set an example for the believers in speech, in life, in love, in faith and in purity. Until I come, devote yourself to the public reading of Scripture, to preaching and to teaching. Do not neglect your gift, which was given you through a prophetic message when the body of elders laid their hands on you.

Be diligent in these matters; give yourself wholly to them, so that everyone may see your progress. Watch your life and doctrine closely. Persevere in them, because if you do, you will save both yourself and your hearers.

(1 Timothy 4:7–16, NIV)

> **"Don't let anyone look down on you because you are young, but set an example for the believers in speech, in life, in love, in faith and in purity."**
> 1 TIMOTHY 4:12, NIV

Q: How does exercising relate to growing in your relationship with Jesus? How is it different?

Q: What, in your definition, is godliness? Why do you think godliness is so important?

Did you know that maturity is measured not by how many years you've walked the earth, but by the depth of your heart? That's why Paul tells Timothy in this passage that no one should look down on his age. His heart is mature.

Q: In what areas of your life do you feel mature? Where do you need to grow up?

Q: How has God gifted you? When others compliment your work, what do they point out? When do you feel most alive?

Q: What do you think Paul means by giving "yourself wholly to them, so that everyone may see your progress"? What is one thing you have given yourself wholly to?

read:

That you may walk (live and conduct yourselves) in a manner worthy of the Lord, fully pleasing to Him and desiring to please Him in all things, bearing fruit in every good work and steadily growing and increasing in and by the knowledge of God [with fuller, deeper, and clearer insight, acquaintance, and recognition].

(Colossians 1:10, AMPLIFIED BIBLE)

Q: What does it mean to walk in a manner worthy of Jesus?

Q: When in your life have you grown steadily in your relationship with Jesus? When have you stayed in the same place? When have you pulled away? Why?

You, therefore, must be perfect [growing into complete maturity of godliness in mind and character, having reached the proper height of virtue and integrity], as your heavenly Father is perfect.

(Matthew 5:48, AMPLIFIED BIBLE)

Q: This is the Amplified Bible. How does the bracketed definition of "perfect" help you understand what it means to follow Jesus apart from your parents?

And other seed [of the same kind] fell into good (well-adapted) soil and brought forth grain, growing up and increasing, and yielded up to thirty times as much, and sixty times as much, and even a hundred times as much as had been sown.

(Mark 4:8, AMPLIFIED BIBLE)

Q: How do you think some people grow in their faith so much and others don't seem to grow at all?

We have much to say about this, but it is hard to explain because you are slow to learn. In fact, though by this time you ought to be teachers, you need someone to teach you the elementary truths of God's word all over again. You need milk, not solid food! Anyone who lives on milk, being still an infant, is not acquainted with the teaching about righteousness. But solid food is for the mature, who by constant use have trained themselves to distinguish good from evil.

(Hebrews 5:11–14, NIV)

Q: As you prepare to leave the home, your parents most likely want you to be mature in your faith. How mature do you feel concerning your relationship with Jesus right now?

Q: In what ways are you still drinking milk?

Q: What, in your opinion, is the "meat" of Christianity?

How mature do you feel concerning your relationship with Jesus right now?

Then we will no longer be infants, tossed back and forth by the waves, and blown here and there by every wind of teaching and by the cunning and craftiness of men in their deceitful scheming.

(Ephesians 4:14, NIV)

Q: According to this verse, what kinds of danger to your faith lurk out in the world?

Q: How can you prepare yourself so you won't be tossed around by all sorts of ideas? In what ways have you already experienced some tossing? Where are ideas being tossed about in your world? (Think: friends talking about stuff, magazine articles, music, etc.)

Talk. ←——————————————————

Activity: How to deal.

Supplies needed:
- A brown paper bag
- Negative and positive traits, cut into strips. Here are some examples:

  - Impatience
  - Joy
  - Wastefulness
  - Curiosity
  - Laziness
  - Sleeping in
  - Overeating
  - Undereating
  - Chattiness
  - People pleasing
  - Authenticity
  - Trustworthiness

Send the bag around. Each person picks out two or three traits, then shares them with the group. Discuss a strategy to deal with their traits that will be helpful to have when they leave home.

Q: What trait seemed to be the worst or the hardest to work around? Which was the most beneficial?

Q: What traits do you struggle with? What trait do you most need?

Q: List the traits currently packed in your bag. Be honest, at least with yourself.

Ricky said, "I have a little more perspective now. I went away to college last year and I actually found myself missing the fam a lot more than I thought I would. That was kind of a shock because when I was living at home, I could not wait to get out."

Q: Do you worry about leaving home? Are you looking forward to it? Why or why not? Is it even possible that it could be different from what you anticipate?

Q: What do you think will be the most exciting part about being on your own? The scariest part?

Libby got frustrated that her mom was packing her bag for camp. And yet she was not packing things that would help her, or even anything she really needed.

Q: Have you ever felt that way? That you could make your own decisions, only to discover your parents actually had some wise advice?

Q: How is your faith your own? In what ways is it exactly the same as your parents?

Q: Think of someone several years older than you with a vibrant faith. What about his/her faith do you admire? Why? Any ideas of how it became "his/her own"?

Do you worry about leaving home? Are you looking forward to it?

 Pray. ⟵—————————————————————

⭐ Activity: Dry-erase prayers.

(This can be as inexpensive as you'd like. Purchase small dry-erase boards or chalkboards at a local dollar store to keep it affordable.)

Supplies needed:
- Enough dry-erase boards or chalkboards for each person in your group. (If you don't have time or resources, give everyone a piece of 8 1/2" x 11" card stock.)
- Pens or chalk.

Show participants an example like the following:

Date	Request	Answer
6/5	Dad's medical tests	

Write seven to ten requests in this way, with today's date on the left-hand side, the request in the middle, and a blank space for God's answer. Since we're talking about parents, growing up, and siblings, let's target the requests to those specific areas.

In a large circle, have each person share one request he/she has listed. End by having each person pray for the request of the person on the left.

Everyone is free to keep their boards. Encourage them to keep them someplace where they'll see their requests daily. It's a tangible way to see God answer prayers. Be sure to follow up next week with God's answers.

You can also keep a chart like this in your journal or wherever you are writing your notes from the study. This will allow for more privacy and a more personal approach.

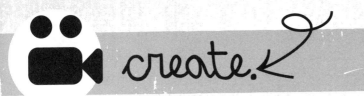

create.

Activity: chart your life through song.

Look back on your life, and try to remember something you were feeling or doing each year from the time you were in first grade until right now, or recall earlier memories if you are able.

Here comes the hard part. Find a song you listened to each year of your life. It doesn't have to have been released in that year, but it has to be one you loved.

It's not easy to create a playlist like this. You may want to text a few friends and ask them what songs they remember. And some of the songs might be really funny (like the *Arthur* theme song from PBS) and some might be downright embarrassing (like your Jonas Brothers stage).

So have at it! Create a playlist of your life starting at first grade and ending with your current grade, one song per year.

When you finish, answer the following questions about your list:

Q: **What years were the hardest to remember in terms of picking songs?**

Q: **What is your favorite song on the list? What about the song makes you love it so much? Are there any that make you sad? Why?**

Q: **How can you see growth in your life over the past decade or so?**

Q: **How has your music taste changed?**

Q: **Can you see any spiritual growth through the changing song selections? Why or why not?**

Q: **What was your favorite song five years ago? What is it today? How are you more emotionally mature than you were five years ago?**

> *Find a song you listened to each year of your life. It doesn't have to have been released in that year, but it has to be one you loved.*

deep.

on your own study #2.

Ricky said some interesting things at the end of the drama while thinking back over his bag and Libby's.

He said, "For Libby it was about her pajamas and candy. And for me it had been about my values and faith. What someone else wants us to bring just won't cut it because we have to wear it when we get there. My parents' values are great. They've taught me a lot—but unless I pack them in my bag myself, they're not going to be real. Just like some of Libby's friends did for camp, I saw a lot of people bring to college all that their parents wanted them to, and then just throw it away when they got there. It takes a lot more courage to hang in there and commit to who you want to be."

> **What are your parents' values? In other words, in the way they live their lives, what do they place high value on?**

Q: What are your parents' values? In other words, in the way they live their lives, what do they place high value on?

Q: How would you rate your parents' relationship with Jesus? Really close? Distant? A mixture?

Q: Right now, how do you see your faith differing from your parents'? Your friends'? Your siblings'?

Q: What one thing have you done in the past year that shows you've owned your faith, made it your own?

Q: What is your biggest fear in leaving home someday in terms of your faith?

read:

Who may worship in your sanctuary, LORD?
   Who may enter your presence on your holy hill?
Those who lead blameless lives and do what is right,
   speaking the truth from sincere hearts.

Those who refuse to gossip
or harm their neighbors
or speak evil of their friends.
Those who despise flagrant sinners,
and honor the faithful followers of the LORD,
and keep their promises even when it hurts.
Those who lend money without charging interest,
and who cannot be bribed to lie about the innocent.
Such people will stand firm forever.
(Psalm 15, NLT)

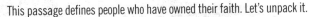

Why is gossip a sin? Did you realize you can gossip about your family too?

This passage defines people who have owned their faith. Let's unpack it.

Q: What does it mean to live a blameless life?

Q: Look back over your week. In what ways have you led a blameless life?

Q: Can you give an example of a time when you did "what was right" in school the past year? What happened? How do you determine what is right and what is wrong?

Q: What would it look like in your life if everyone you knew refused to gossip?

Q: Why is gossip a sin? Did you realize you can gossip about your family too?

Q: What does it mean to bring harm to your neighbors (your friends and the people around you)?

Q: When was the last time a friend "spoke evil" of you? How did it feel? Why do you think speaking evil of someone is something God doesn't like?

Q: How would you feel if your parents spoke evil of you in front of their friends? How would they feel if they heard some of your complaints about them?

Q: What does it mean to "despise flagrant sinners"? Does this mean you're supposed to hate anyone who isn't a Jesus follower? Why or why not? (Hint: the definition of flagrant is "obvious, offensive, blatant, scandalous, outrageously bad.")

Q: When was the last time you "honor[ed] the faithful followers of the LORD"? What does that mean? When have you felt honored by someone? What did he/she do to honor you?

When you leave home, you'll be tempted to let go of your integrity (your insides and outsides matching; you do what you say you'll do). Keeping a promise might hurt or be too hard. But Psalm 15:4 says those who grow in God will "keep their promises even when it hurts."

Q: When was the last time one of your parents let you down, in terms of their promises? What happened? How did you feel?

Q: When have you kept a promise even when it cost you dearly? What happened?

You may have heard it said that a person's heart is connected to his/her wallet. Or that you'll know people's relationship with God by what they do with their money. Jesus said our heart is where our treasure is.

Q: How have you seen your parents be generous? In what ways do people demonstrate generosity?

Q: What do you like about the way your parents manage their money? Is there anything you would change about how they handle finances?

Q: What lessons do you want to take away from your parents in terms of money? What do you want to do differently?

The end of the psalm says the folks who follow all those paths (integrity, honesty, kindness, generosity) "will stand firm forever."

Q: Over the last year, how have you stood firm in your faith?

Q: In what ways have you waffled?

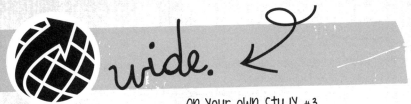

wide.

What do You Wear?

Let's look at some "clothing" verses.

read:

Let no debt remain outstanding, except the continuing debt to love one another, for he who loves his fellowman has fulfilled the law. The commandments, "Do not commit adultery," "Do not murder," "Do not steal," "Do not covet," and whatever other commandment there may be, are summed up in this one rule: "Love your neighbor as yourself." Love does no harm to its neighbor. Therefore love is the fulfillment of the law.

And do this, understanding the present time. The hour has come for you to wake up from your slumber, because our salvation is nearer now than when we first believed. The night is nearly over; the day is almost here. So let us put aside the deeds of darkness and **put on** *the armor of light. Let us behave decently, as in the daytime, not in orgies and drunkenness, not in sexual immorality and debauchery, not in dissension and jealousy. Rather,* **clothe yourselves** *with the Lord Jesus Christ, and do not think about how to gratify the desires of the sinful nature.*

> **"Love does no harm to its neighbor. Therefore love is the fulfillment of the law."**
> ROMANS 13:10, NIV

(Romans 13:8–14, NIV, emphasis added)

This verse talks about clothing yourself with Jesus. In other words, you'll want to put Jesus in your bag as you pack for the life outside your childhood home.

Q: **What do the verses above the "clothe yourself with Jesus" part deal with primarily? (Hint: read the first sentence.)**

Q: **How do you love your parents as yourself? In what ways is it easy to ignore that commandment in your relationship with your parents? Your siblings?**

Q: **What would your parents say is your greatest conflict with them? How can you clothe yourself with Jesus in that conflict?**

Q: What would change if you and everyone in your house loved one another in the same way they loved themselves?

Q: What is one specific way you can put your parents above yourself this week? Ask a friend to hold you accountable to doing that.

read:

A final word: Be strong in the Lord and in his mighty power. **Put on** *all of God's armor so that you will be able to stand firm against all strategies of the devil. For we are not fighting against flesh-and-blood enemies, but against evil rulers and authorities of the unseen world, against mighty powers in this dark world, and against evil spirits in the heavenly places.*

Therefore, **put on** *every piece of God's armor so you will be able to resist the enemy in the time of evil. Then after the battle you will still be standing firm. Stand your ground,* **putting on** *the belt of truth and the body armor of God's righteousness. For shoes,* **put on** *the peace that comes from the Good News so that you will be fully prepared. In addition to all of these, hold up the shield of faith to stop the fiery arrows of the devil.* **Put on** *salvation as your helmet, and take the sword of the Spirit, which is the word of God.*

Pray in the Spirit at all times and on every occasion. Stay alert and be persistent in your prayers for all believers everywhere.

(Ephesians 6:10–18, NLT, emphasis added)

Sometimes when you have conflict with your parents, you see them as the enemy. Yet this Scripture says that the real enemy is not them at all, but the devil and his evil schemes.

> *Sometimes when you have conflict with your parents, you see them as the enemy. Yet Scripture says that the real enemy is not them at all, but the devil and his evil schemes.*

Q: How could putting on the armor of God (truth, righteousness, peace, faith, salvation, Word of God, prayer) help you deal with frustrations with your parents?

Q: How does knowing your true conflict is not with people, but with the devil, help you interact with your parents when things are rough?

Q: When was the last time you prayed for your parents? What did you pray?

Likewise, you who are younger, be subject to the elders. **Clothe yourselves**, *all of you, with humility toward one another, for "God opposes the proud but gives grace to the humble."*

Humble yourselves, therefore, under the mighty hand of God so that at the proper time he may exalt you, casting all your anxieties on him, because he cares for you.

(1 Peter 5:5–7, ᴇsᴠ, emphasis added)

Humility means sometimes letting others win. It means listening to someone telling you you're in the wrong—and then changing. It means looking at yourself realistically.

Q: **In what ways are you humble with your parents?**

Q: **Would your parents say you are humble? When would they be most likely to see you acting that way?**

Q: **What does this Scripture say about humility? Who are you first to humble yourself before?**

Q: **What happens when you try to get your own way (pride) in terms of your relationship with God?**

This verse talks about submitting to your elders. While this is referring to elders in the church, there are plenty of other Scriptures about the importance of children obeying their parents. But sometimes it's hard to obey, isn't it? Sometimes parents try to hold you back into childhood.

Q: **In what ways do your parents try to hold you back? Why do you think they do this?**

Q: **How, exactly, are they afraid to let you grow up? What might happen?**

Q: **How would you rate your communication with your parents over the last year on a scale from 1 (lowest) to 10 (highest)? Why did you give it that rating?**

Q: **How can you improve the communication between you and your parents? What kinds of traits do you need to "put on"?**

Activity: Put it down on paper.

Write out a prayer about your relationship with your parents—your hopes, frustrations, desires, and fears. Ask Jesus to come into the midst of your conflicts. Ask Him to help you clothe yourself with humility.

Prayer:

_____

_____

_____

_____

_____

_____

_____

_____

_____

_____

_____

_____

_____

_____

_____

_____

_____

_____

_____

_____

_____

dare.

Activity: "Dear Me."

In a quiet place with a piece of stationery, write yourself a letter in two parts.

Part one: Write a letter to a younger you, telling yourself what you've learned so far in life. Warn younger you about upcoming choices, and let him/her know what wisdom you've gained. Concentrate on how you've grown or fallen off in your relationship with Jesus, how well or badly you think you've handled peer pressure, what you've learned about getting along with others. You may even tackle money, gossip, friendships, and how you worship.

Part two: Write a letter to the you that you hope to be in seven years. Tell yourself what you'd like to hold on to in terms of your faith. How would you like to see yourself? Will you be attending college? Have a job? What kind? Will you be pursuing your dreams? How? What will your walk with Christ look like then? What kind of advice will you offer your older self?

Now, seal this letter in an envelope. On the front write "Don't open until _____," then date the letter seven years from today. Keep it in a safe place, maybe in the back of your Bible, or in a box of memories.

Fun, crazy dare:

Ask one of your parents to pick your clothes for tomorrow, then surprise him/her by wearing the outfit!

Ask one of your parents to pick your clothes for tomorrow, then surprise him or her by wearing the outfit!

Resources & iTunes List

Resources.

- *Toy Story 3* (movie)
- *Freaks and Geeks* (TV)
- *Strictly Ballroom* (movie)
- *The Wonder Years* (TV)

 ## Listen. ←

- "Day after Day" by Tim Hughes, *Here I Am to Worship*
- "Walk On" by U2, *All That You Can't Leave Behind*
- "Show Me What I'm Looking For" by Carolina Liar, *Coming to Terms*
- "Stop and Stare" by OneRepublic, *Dreaming Out Loud*
- "Happy Together" by The Turtles, *The Turtles*
- "Come Along" by Titiyo, *Come Along*
- "Late Have I Loved You" by Gungor, *Beautiful Things*

one choice

BRIEF OUTTAKE: Sophie makes a choice to attend a "party" where she ends up having sex with Jason. She wonders what her life would've been like had she accepted Patrick's invitation to go to the fair for a carefree time. After finding out she's pregnant, she's faced with another choice, but the drama doesn't tell us which choice she makes.

 watch dvd episode 3.

 Group Study:

 Truth.

Go around your circle and share the answer to these questions (and remember to tell the truth!):

Q: When was the last time you had a choice between two evenings—one that was "safe" and one that wasn't? What did you choose? Why? Did you have any regrets?

Q: What's a recent choice you've made that you are proud of?

Q: How much time did it take for Sophie to make her choice? How long will she live out the consequences of that choice?

Q: What choice do you think she made at the end of the sketch? Why?

Read Gregg's Story:

It's funny how you sometimes can't see God until after the fact. Before I stepped into that car, I knew something. I knew I shouldn't go with Jake, Sarah, and Brody. I could smell the pot as they asked me to get in the car. I ignored that voice inside me that told me to walk away. I guess I wanted to be cool. So I hopped in.

At first, just driving around was fun. Our music blasted with the windows wide open and we sang really loud. Brody yelled at this old lady on the side of the road, startling her. The three of them laughed that "we're all high" laugh, and I slumped down in the backseat. The lady looked rattled.

Then Jake started driving faster. It was a game to him to see how fast he could go over the limit. I gripped my seat belt, then closed my eyes. The wind blew, the music blared, and I wanted to find a way to shout to someone to drop me off at the next light.

> *Before I could shout my answer, the car spun wildly out of control. I saw the telephone pole in the headlight beam, but I couldn't stop it from coming our way.*

"What's wrong with you?" Sarah poked me and yelled in my face.

Before I could shout my answer, the car spun wildly out of control. I saw the telephone pole in the headlight beam, but I couldn't stop it from coming our way. The crash deafened me. Sarah and I were belted in, and when everything finally stopped moving, she just stared at me, bloody-eyed, in shock. I looked into the front seat, and couldn't see Jake. Brody mouthed, "He's not here," then pointed outside.

Jake didn't die, thank God. But he had a concussion, lost his spleen, and stayed in the hospital for three weeks. He can't play football anymore because the doctor worries he'll get another concussion, and if he does, it could do some serious damage. He also was cited for driving while impaired, which means he can't drive for a long time. He totaled his car. His parents refuse to replace it.

Brody seems unfazed by the whole thing, just laughs it off if you ask him about it.

Sarah won't talk to any of us. It's like she's still in some state of shock. The gash on the side of her face is gone, but she has a pretty bad scar. She's gotten really thin the past few months.

And me? I'm grateful to be alive. I still can't believe I got in that car. So stupid. One choice that could have cost me everything. For some reason, I think God spared me, gave me the chance to learn and listen to that "voice" the next time.

Q: Have you ever had an experience like Gregg's or do you know someone who has?

Q: Why did Gregg get in the car? Was it a valid reason?

Q: How is Sarah coping with the stress of the accident? Brody?

Q: What were some of the direct consequences of Jake's accident for Jake?

 word. ←——————————————————————————

 read:

In the spring, at the time when kings go off to war, David sent Joab out with the king's men and the whole Israelite army. They destroyed the Ammonites and besieged Rabbah. But David remained in Jerusalem.

One evening David got up from his bed and walked around on the roof of the palace. From the roof he saw a woman bathing. The woman was very beautiful, and David sent someone to find out about her. The man said, "Isn't this Bathsheba, the daughter of Eliam and the wife of Uriah the Hittite?" Then David sent messengers to get her. She came to him, and he slept with her. (She had purified herself from her uncleanness.) Then she went back home. The woman conceived and sent word to David, saying, "I am pregnant."

So David sent this word to Joab: "Send me Uriah the Hittite." And Joab sent him to David. When Uriah came to him, David asked him how Joab was, how the soldiers were and how the war was going. Then David said to Uriah, "Go down to your house and wash your feet." So Uriah left the palace, and a gift from the king was sent after him. But Uriah slept at the entrance to the palace with all his master's servants and did not go down to his house.

When David was told, "Uriah did not go home," he asked him, "Haven't you just come from a distance? Why didn't you go home?"

Uriah said to David, "The ark and Israel and Judah are staying in tents, and my master Joab and my lord's men are camped in the open fields. How could I go to my house to eat and drink and lie with my wife? As surely as you live, I will not do such a thing!"

Then David said to him, "Stay here one more day, and tomorrow I will send you back." So Uriah remained in Jerusalem that day and the next. At David's invitation, he ate and drank with him, and David made him drunk. But in the evening Uriah went out to sleep on his mat among his master's servants; he did not go home.

In the morning David wrote a letter to Joab and sent it with Uriah. In it he wrote, "Put Uriah in the front line where the fighting is fiercest. Then withdraw from him so he will be struck down and die."

So while Joab had the city under siege, he put Uriah at a place where he knew the strongest defenders were. When the men of the city came out and fought against Joab, some of the men in David's army fell; moreover, Uriah the Hittite died.

David made many destructive choices . . . but it all started with one choice.

Joab sent David a full account of the battle. He instructed the messenger: "When you have finished giving the king this account of the battle, the king's anger may flare up, and he may ask you, 'Why did you get so close to the city to fight? Didn't you know they would shoot arrows from the wall? Who killed Abimelech son of Jerub-Besheth? Didn't a woman throw an upper millstone on him from the wall, so that he died in Thebez? Why did you get so close to the wall?' If he asks you this, then say to him, 'Also, your servant Uriah the Hittite is dead.'"

The messenger set out, and when he arrived he told David everything Joab had sent him to say. The messenger said to David, "The men overpowered us and came out against us in the open, but we drove them back to the entrance to the city gate. Then the archers shot arrows at your servants from the wall, and some of the king's men died. Moreover, your servant Uriah the Hittite is dead."

David told the messenger, "Say this to Joab: 'Don't let this upset you; the sword devours one as well as another. Press the attack against the city and destroy it.' Say this to encourage Joab."

When Uriah's wife heard that her husband was dead, she mourned for him.

(2 Samuel 11:1–26, NIV)

David made many destructive choices in the biblical account above, but it all started with one choice.

Q: **What was his first choice in this series of devastating choices?**

Q: **When have you made a choice based on boredom or laziness?**

Q: **Did Bathsheba ask for David's advances?**

David was able to make certain choices because of his position as king. He abused his power. Today's headlines on CNN are full of such examples. Which recent ones come to mind?

Q: **Have you known someone in your life who made a choice based on his/her power over someone else? What happened?**

After David slept with Bathsheba, she sent word to him that she was pregnant.

Q: **How did David respond? Why do you think he did this?**

Often we think our choices have nothing to do with anyone else, that they are ours alone to make. And yet, after reading David's story, we see many others whose lives were deeply affected by his choice.

Q: **Who were the people most hurt by David's choices? (There are at least four.)**

Q: **David staged a massive cover-up, even though he was the king and could get away with whatever he wanted. Why was he hiding what he had done? Does hiding work? (You'll look at this in depth later this week.)**

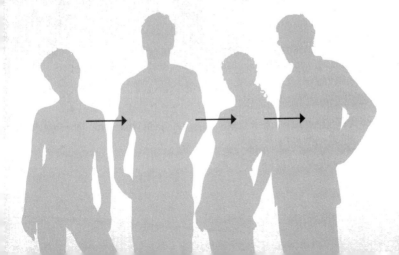

Talk. ←————————————————————

Activity: Paper covers rock.

Play rock, paper, scissors in groups of two; best out of five wins. Play until you have an overall winner.

Rock, paper, scissors is a silly game we've played since childhood. But when you think about it, even choices made on the fly can have huge consequences. Our choices matter. Little ones, big ones, medium ones. Each one changes the course of our lives.

> *When you think about it, even choices made on the fly can have huge consequences.*

Q: What are the seemingly silly choices you've made that had a huge impact later?

Q: What decisions seemed huge at the time, but then didn't seem to matter in the grand scheme of things?

Q: Look back over your day. What is one small choice you made that ended up making a huge difference today.

Q: Look back over your month. What is one huge choice you made? What happened after the choice?

The narrator in the sketch you watched said, "Have you ever wondered about the real consequences of one choice? If I go this way, what will happen, or if I don't get in that car on that night, how will my life really be different? If we could see the end result, would it affect the choices we make?"

Q: Look back over a choice you made that had a painful result. If you had known what would've happened, would you still have made that choice? Why or why not?

Sophie, after sleeping with Jason, said, "I just made one choice, and then it seemed like the next few choices were just made for me."

Q: Thinking back on David's life, how did things spiral out of control for him? How did they spiral out of control for Sophie?

Q: What choices seemed out of control?

Jason told Sophie: "Nothing. You haven't done anything. You don't have to feel bad about this. They just like to scare us all the time. Ooooh, it's so bad; it's so wrong. C'mon, that's not how you feel now, is it?"

Q: **Why do you think Jason didn't feel bad about what happened? Do you think he was telling the truth? If not, what was he covering up?**

Jason offered to take Sophie to a movie to get her mind off things.

Q: **Is it helpful to forget about your stress by escaping into a movie or TV show? Why or why not? When was the last time you "escaped"?**

Jason called what they did "a stupid mistake," but it involved deliberate choices by both of them.

Jason called what they did "a stupid mistake," but it involved deliberate choices by both of them. He said, "Why did I invite her over anyway? It wasn't even all that great. So stupid, stupid, stupid."

Q: **Why do you think Jason didn't take ownership of his part of the problem? Based on what he said, was he blaming Sophie? How?**

Q: **What was Jason's solution to Sophie's pregnancy? What did it cost him?**

Q: **Are the consequences of sex the same for guys and girls?**

Q: **Sophie faced two choices at the end. What were they?**

Activity: Postcards to God.

Supplies needed:
- A postcard for each person
- Pens
- Creative stamps or stickers

Write a prayer to God based on one of the choices you've made in the last year (either positive or negative). This is a private prayer exercise. Keep the time quiet and reflective. Here are some examples if you're having a hard time figuring out what to write:

Positive choice: *Dear God, thank You for giving me the strength to say no to the kid in band who offered me pot the first day of practice. Part of me wanted to fit in right away, but I'm so thankful You gave me the ability and desire to say a big, fat no. Help me in the future to listen to Your voice.*

> Dear God, thank You for giving me the strength to say no to the kid in band who offered me pot the first day of practice.

Negative choice: *Jesus, I'm sorry for glancing over at Natasha's paper during the chemistry test yesterday. I knew I shouldn't have done it. Please forgive me. Help me to change, to not be so consumed with grades that I lose sight of my choices. Please help me not cheat.*

(Note to leader: Have your group place their postcards into an envelope and seal it. A month or so later, mail the postcard back to your group with this verse on the backside:

"Then you will call upon me and come and pray to me, and I will listen to you. You will seek me and find me when you seek me with all your heart. I will be found by you," declares the LORD, *"and will bring you back from captivity. I will gather you from all the nations and places where I have banished you," declares the* LORD, *"and will bring you back to the place from which I carried you into exile."*

(Jeremiah 29:12–14, NIV)

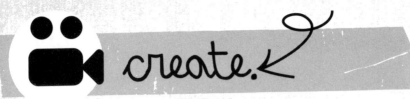

create.

on your own study #1.

ACTiViTY: The end.

You've talked about what might've happened at the end of the drama. Now it's your turn to write the ending. You can either write it on your computer or in the pages of your journal (if you have one).

Remember, there is a lag time between Jason giving Sophie the money and her coming home to her parents. What happened between? You might also want to include Patrick, the guy who invited Sophie to the fair. Or you can add new characters. Whatever you choose is great.

Speculate. Ponder. Create. End this story the way you think it should end.

The end:

_____

_____

_____

_____

_____

_____

_____

_____

_____

_____

_____

_____

_____

_____

_____

_____

MariJuana

BY TODD M. CLEMENTS, M.D.

Today more than five thousand teenagers will try marijuana for the first time. That's more than one hundred school buses completely filled with guys and girls who are about to roll the dice to experiment with something that could cost them everything. What's mind-blowing is that the same thing will happen tomorrow and the next day and the next day. Some will only try it once, but many will use it again, and some will start to use it on a daily basis. Marijuana is the most prevalent illegal drug used in high schools today.[1]

Teens report they use marijuana mainly because it makes them feel relaxed and decreases worry. Some say they smoke it before parties because it helps them feel less anxious and uptight about talking to other people. Some people say it just makes them giggly and laugh at everything, while others say the only reason they use it is because their friends do. In fact, some teens say they don't even like it, but are afraid they won't be socially accepted if they don't use it.

What disturbs me deeply when I talk to teens who use marijuana is how unaware they are of its dangers. Almost all will tell me things they've heard from their friends, like, it isn't harmful, it's not addictive, it's better than alcohol, and so on. Sadly, these teenagers don't know what research tells us is the truth about marijuana.

There are well-documented studies that show using marijuana can lead to depression, anxiety, panic attacks, and paranoia (the feeling that other people are against you or out to cause you harm). Some users even hallucinate (hear voices when no one is there or see things that aren't real). There are cases where the hallucinations and paranoia continue for years—even after quitting marijuana. Studies also show that marijuana worsens your memory.[2]

It's likely someone will try to persuade you to smoke marijuana if it hasn't happened already. While it may seem harmless and fun, I've seen the ugly sides of this drug, and my role as a doctor is to tell you the truth: it is not harmless—its effects can alter your brain and change your life in negative ways.

Dr. Todd Clements *is a board-certified psychiatrist and is the medical director of the Clements Clinic in Plano, Texas.*

1 Richard K. Rikes, M.D., Shannon C. Miller, M.D., David A. Fiellen, M.D., and Richard Saitz, M.D., *Principles of Addiction Medicine*, 4th ed., (Philadelphia: Abuse Lippincott Williams & Wilkins, 2007), 1367.
2 Ibid., 1139-49.

on your own study #2.

Does hiding work?

read:

The LORD sent Nathan to David. When he came to him, he said, "There were two men in a certain town, one rich and the other poor. The rich man had a very large number of sheep and cattle, but the poor man had nothing except one little ewe lamb he had bought. He raised it, and it grew up with him and his children. It shared his food, drank from his cup and even slept in his arms. It was like a daughter to him.

"Now a traveler came to the rich man, but the rich man refrained from taking one of his own sheep or cattle to prepare a meal for the traveler who had come to him. Instead, he took the ewe lamb that belonged to the poor man and prepared it for the one who had come to him."

David burned with anger against the man and said to Nathan, "As surely as the LORD lives, the man who did this deserves to die! He must pay for that lamb four times over, because he did such a thing and had no pity."

Then Nathan said to David, "You are the man! This is what the LORD, the God of Israel, says: 'I anointed you king over Israel, and I delivered you from the hand of Saul. I gave your master's house to you, and your master's wives into your arms. I gave you the house of Israel and Judah. And if all this had been too little, I would have given you even more. Why did you despise the word of the LORD by doing what is evil in his eyes? You struck down Uriah the Hittite with the sword and took his wife to be your own. You killed him with the sword of the Ammonites. Now, therefore, the sword will never depart from your house, because you despised me and took the wife of Uriah the Hittite to be your own.'

"This is what the LORD says: 'Out of your own household I am going to bring calamity upon you. Before your very eyes I will take your wives and give them to one who is close to you, and he will lie with your wives in broad daylight. You did it in secret, but I will do this thing in broad daylight before all Israel.'"

Then David said to Nathan, "I have sinned against the LORD."

(2 Samuel 12:1–13a, NIV)

David "got away with" his decision to have sex with a woman who wasn't his wife. Or so he thought. Isn't it interesting that David was called a man after God's own heart, yet he somehow thought he could pull the wool over God's eyes? As if God couldn't see exactly what he did? But God did see, and He let Nathan in on David's secret.

Q: Did Nathan directly confront David? What do you think would've happened had Nathan just pointed out David's sin?

Q: Nathan demonstrated just how powerful a story can be. What story did he tell?

Q: How did David respond?

Q: How is David's reaction ironic?

Q: What scary words did Nathan say to David?

Q: What consequences did Nathan tell David God would bring?

> David "got away with" his decision to have sex with a woman who wasn't his wife. Or so he thought.

Often when we're confronted with our choices, our fallback is to push back and keep hiding. To deny. To holler. To discredit the messenger. It's what we see and read about every day in the stories of "fallen" politicians, sports figures, and others. But David doesn't do that.

Q: What was David's reaction?

Q: How do you think Jason (from the drama) would respond to someone like Nathan in his life? What about Sophie? What story could Nathan have told Jason to help him see his sin?

The devastation of the choices made affected David and his whole kingdom, and we get a glimpse of the pain to come in Sophie's life as a result of the choices she made.

Q: How do you think having an abortion affects the heart of a girl who has one?

Q: How does providing money for an abortion affect the heart of the father of the unborn child?

Q: Is there such a thing as a choice that results in no consequences? If a choice is good or sinful, does that affect the consequences that follow? Why or why not?

Q: Will hiding a sinful choice mean you don't experience the consequences if no one finds out?

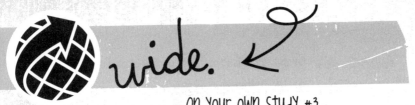

read:

Nathan replied, "The Lord has taken away your sin. You are not going to die. But because by doing this you have made the enemies of the Lord show utter contempt, the son born to you will die."

After Nathan had gone home, the Lord struck the child that Uriah's wife had borne to David, and he became ill. David pleaded with God for the child. He fasted and went into his house and spent the nights lying on the ground. The elders of his household stood beside him to get him up from the ground, but he refused, and he would not eat any food with them.

On the seventh day the child died. David's servants were afraid to tell him that the child was dead, for they thought, "While the child was still living, we spoke to David but he would not listen to us. How can we tell him the child is dead? He may do something desperate."

David noticed that his servants were whispering among themselves and he realized the child was dead. "Is the child dead?" he asked.

"Yes," they replied, "he is dead."

Then David got up from the ground. After he had washed, put on lotions and changed his clothes, he went into the house of the Lord and worshiped. Then he went to his own house, and at his request they served him food, and he ate.

His servants asked him, "Why are you acting this way? While the child was alive, you fasted and wept, but now that the child is dead, you get up and eat!"

He answered, "While the child was still alive, I fasted and wept. I thought, 'Who knows? The Lord may be gracious to me and let the child live.' But now that he is dead, why should I fast? Can I bring him back again? I will go to him, but he will not return to me."

Then David comforted his wife Bathsheba, and he went to her and lay with her. She gave birth to a son, and they named him Solomon. The Lord loved him; and because the Lord loved him, he sent word through Nathan the prophet to name him Jedidiah.

(2 Samuel 12:13b–25, NIV)

Q: What were some of the consequences of David's series of choices?

Still, David believed in God's grace and ability to pardon.

Q: What did he do while his son was sick? Why do you think he did this?

Q: What was the first thing David did when he heard about his son's death? What was the second thing he did?

When we begin to see the consequences of our own sinful choices, we have new choices to make. We can run from God, feeling way too ashamed to try to deal with what we've done. Or we can humble ourselves and ask God for a second chance, which is what David did.

David wrote after Nathan confronted him:

read:

Generous in love—God, give grace! Huge
*   in mercy—wipe out my bad record.*
Scrub away my guilt,
*   soak out my sins in your laundry.*
I know how bad I've been;
*   my sins are staring me down.*

You're the One I've violated, and you've seen
*   it all, seen the full extent of my evil.*
You have all the facts before you;
*   whatever you decide about me is fair.*
I've been out of step with you for a long time,
*   in the wrong since before I was born.*
What you're after is truth from the inside out.
*   Enter me, then; conceive a new, true life.*

Soak me in your laundry and I'll come out clean,
*   scrub me and I'll have a snow-white life.*
Tune me in to foot-tapping songs,
*   set these once-broken bones to dancing.*
Don't look too close for blemishes,
*   give me a clean bill of health.*

God, make a fresh start in me,
*   shape a Genesis week from the chaos of my life.*
Don't throw me out with the trash,
*   or fail to breathe holiness in me.*
Bring me back from gray exile,
*   put a fresh wind in my sails!*
Give me a job teaching rebels your ways
*   so the lost can find their way home.*
Commute my death sentence, God, my salvation God,
*   and I'll sing anthems to your life-giving ways.*
Unbutton my lips, dear God;
*   I'll let loose with your praise.*

Going through the motions doesn't please you,
*   a flawless performance is nothing to you.*
I learned God-worship
*   when my pride was shattered.*
Heart-shattered lives ready for love
*   don't for a moment escape God's notice.*

Make Zion the place you delight in,
*   repair Jerusalem's broken-down walls.*
Then you'll get real worship from us,
*   acts of worship small and large,*
Including all the bulls
*   they can heave onto your altar!*
*   (Psalm 51, MSG)*

> When we begin to see the consequences of our own sinful choices, we have new choices to make. We can run from God, feeling way too ashamed to try to deal with what we've done. Or we can humble ourselves and ask God for a second chance.

Q: Circle the places where you see God's ability to wash David clean.

Q: Put a square around the places where David worships.

Q: Although David sinned against Bathsheba, Uriah, and a host of others, who does he say he ultimately has sinned against?

David told God that he made the wrong choice (admitted his sin), then repented before God (turned away from his sin). He let God wash his soul. Then he worshipped. Even after his failure, David realized that God had still more ways to use his life. He wrote, "Give me a job teaching rebels your ways so the lost can find their way home."

Q: How did David move on? What job did God give him?

Q: How could David teach people God's ways after he sinned? And why might he do a better job of it? Why would God use a broken man?

Q: How can brokenness be a benefit?

In 2 Corinthians 12:9–10, Paul talks about boasting about his weakness so that the power of Jesus can be strong in him. Did you realize that when you are strong and self-sufficient, God can't work through you? It's when you're at the end of your rope, helpless and needy, that God can truly do His best work. If you've made a bad choice, remember that Jesus loves you. He can clean you. He can use you more in your state of brokenness than when you were doing fine in your own strength. Be encouraged.

dare.

Read this psalm and notice the bolded parts, which deal with choices.

read:

I bless God every chance I get; my lungs expand with his praise.

I live and breathe God;
if things aren't going well, hear this and be happy:

Join me in spreading the news;
together let's get the word out.

God met me more than halfway,
he freed me from my anxious fears.

Look at him; give him your warmest smile.
Never hide your feelings from him.

When I was desperate, I called out,
and God got me out of a tight spot.

God's angel sets up a circle
of protection around us while we pray.

Open your mouth and taste, open your eyes and see—
       how good God is.
Blessed are you who run to him.

Worship God if you want the best;
worship opens doors to all his goodness.

Young lions on the prowl get hungry,
but God-seekers are full of God.

Come, children, listen closely;
I'll give you a lesson in God worship.

Who out there has a lust for life?
Can't wait each day to come upon beauty?

Guard your tongue from profanity,
and no more lying through your teeth.

Turn your back on sin; do something good.
Embrace peace—don't let it get away!

GOD keeps an eye on his friends,
his ears pick up every moan and groan.

GOD won't put up with rebels;
he'll cull them from the pack.

Is anyone crying for help? GOD is listening,
ready to rescue you.

If your heart is broken, you'll find GOD right there;
if you're kicked in the gut, he'll help you catch your breath.

Disciples so often get into trouble;
still, GOD is there every time.

He's your bodyguard, shielding every bone;
not even a finger gets broken.

The wicked commit slow suicide;
they waste their lives hating the good.

GOD pays for each slave's freedom;
no one who runs to him loses out.

(Psalm 34, MSG)

Q: How has God helped you when you've wanted to make a bad choice? How has He been your bodyguard?

Q: How did God help the person who wrote this psalm? (Side note: David wrote this psalm.)

Q: Even when you've gotten into trouble, the Bible says, "God is there every time." How has God been near when you've felt far away from Him?

The passage says, "Is anyone crying for help? God is listening, ready to rescue you."

If you dare:

1. Dare to admit your sin. Let it out. Write it out if you must. Get it out.
2. Dare to tell God you're sorry.
3. Dare to apologize to those you've hurt.
4. Dare to ask God to wash you squeaky clean.
5. Dare to worship Him, even if you feel small or ashamed.
6. Dare to move on. Do the next thing. Ask God to use this experience to make your heart more open to Him.
7. Dare to keep going.

Even when you've gotten into trouble, the Bible says, "God is there every time."
PSALM 34:19B

Resources & iTunes List

Resources.

- *The New Teen Choices Game*, by FaithKidz
- *Anything but Normal*, by Melody Carlson
- *The 6 Most Important Decisions You'll Ever Make: A Guide for Teens*, by Sean Covey
- *The 7 Habits of Highly Effective Teens*, by Sean Covey
- *Dust* (Nooma video), http://www.nooma.com

 ## Listen. ←

- "Let Your Soul Be Your Pilot" by Sting, *Mercury Falling*
- "This Is Home" by Switchfoot, *The Best Yet*
- "Stop This Train" by John Mayer, *Continuum*
- "Brick" by Ben Folds Five, *Whatever and Ever Amen*

baggage

BRIEF OUTTAKE: Annie carries a lot of bags full of wounds and hurts, collected over the years of her young life—the divorce of her parents, a hurtful relationship, church wounds, and self-image struggles. She has to decide whether she wants to continue to live life weighed down by her burdens or trust that God has provided a way for her to lay it all down.

 watch dvd episode 4.

 Group Study:

 Truth. ←

Go around your circle and share the answer to these questions (and remember to tell the truth!):

Q: What hit you most about this drama?

Q: In what ways is Annie like you? How is she different?

Q: What would your closest friend say you carry that you need to let go of?

Read Sandi's Story:

Other people say I do too much, but I disagree. I don't do nearly enough. It's like I thrive on throwing things in the air and keeping them airborne. The thought of something falling actually excites me, makes me work harder.

I do ballet—and not just any ballet. The best. The kind that requires hours and hours of practice. I get almost perfect grades, because there was that A-, which I'm still angry about. I should've done more extra credit.

> *Staying busy is great for me. I never have time to think. Or I guess I should say feel.*

I told Mom yesterday that I would help with dinner from now on. She's just so busy, working and volunteering, and it's the least I can do. I'll find a way to squeeze it in between my Advanced Placement homework and that movie project I'm working on. Did I mention that I was chosen to be the president of the Spanish Club too? That's really fun and a great honor. I'll be organizing the Cinco de Mayo festival this year. It shouldn't be too hard. A piñata here, some quesadillas, sombreros for everyone.

Staying busy is great for me. I never have time to think. Or I guess I should say feel. I can't stop thinking about all the things I have to do. Which is totally good because I am afraid if I feel, then I'll just collapse. Better not to even go there. So I don't dwell on the divorce or my sister's going off the deep end. Or my dad and how he never shows up like he says. If I just keep super busy, focused on all my stuff, it's as if these other things don't exist.

And that's just fine by me.

Q: **Do you know anyone like Sandi?**

Q: **When was the last time you evaluated your life in terms of what to let go and what to keep?**

Q: **Would you describe yourself as stressed out? Why or why not?**

Word. ←——————————————————

 read:

Be strong and of good courage, do not fear nor be afraid of them; for the LORD your God, He is the One who goes with you. He will not leave you nor forsake you.
(Deuteronomy 31:6, NKJV)

Q: In the drama, "Baggage," did Annie feel strong? Courageous? How would knowing that God would never leave her have helped Annie?

Q: Have you ever felt forsaken by God? When?

Cast your cares on the LORD and he will sustain you; he will never let the righteous fall.
(Psalm 55:22, NIV)

Q: How have you seen your parents "cast their cares" on the Lord? Or have they? Has anyone ever shown you what it would look like to give your cares to God?

The LORD upholds all who fall, and raises up all who are bowed down.
(Psalm 145:14, NKJV)

Q: When was the last time you experienced God lifting you up from a very dark place?

"Forget the former things; do not dwell on the past. See, I am doing a new thing! Now it springs up; do you not perceive it? I am making a way in the desert and streams in the wasteland."
(Isaiah 43:18–19, NIV)

Q: Why do you think Annie couldn't see God's offer to make a way through her over-burdened life?

Q: What would it look like for Annie to experience streams in her wasteland? Do you think she experienced that at the end of the drama? Why or why not?

We are hard pressed on every side, but not crushed; perplexed, but not in despair; persecuted, but not abandoned; struck down, but not destroyed.
(2 Corinthians 4:8–9, NIV)

This is a true verse, but sometimes it doesn't feel true. Sometimes life feels way too painful or stressful. We may feel hard-pressed, crushed, despairing, abandoned, and destroyed.

Q: What do you think the apostle Paul meant by this Scripture?

"Come to me, all you who are weary and burdened, and I will give you rest. Take my yoke upon you and learn from me, for I am gentle and humble in heart, and you will find rest for your souls. For my yoke is easy and my burden is light."

(Matthew 11:28–30, NIV)

Q: What is rest to you? Is sleep the same as rest? Why or why not?

Q: When have you felt the most rested? What brought it about?

> **"Come to me, all you who are weary and burdened, and I will give you rest."**
> MATTHEW 11:28, NIV

Q: What does Jesus ask of those who are weary?

Carry each other's burdens, and in this way you will fulfill the law of Christ. If anyone thinks he is something when he is nothing, he deceives himself. Each one should test his own actions. Then he can take pride in himself, without comparing himself to somebody else, for each one should carry his own load.

(Galatians 6:2–5, NIV)

Q: What does this verse suggest about how we can be free of baggage?

Q: Who in your life has carried your burdens? What did that look like?

Q: How, really, do you carry a friend's burdens? What does that look like?

Some people love to appear like they have everything together, when in reality they're having a difficult time.

Q: Why is it hard to ask others for help?

Q: What is difficult about comparing yourself to others? Why do you think it's harmful?

And I heard a loud voice from the throne, saying, "Now God's presence is with people, and he will live with them, and they will be his people. God himself will be with them and will be their God. He will wipe away every tear from their eyes, and there will be no more death, sadness, crying, or pain, because all the old ways are gone."

(Revelation 21:3–4, NCV)

Eventually, in heaven, we'll have a baggage-less life. No more burdens. No more tears.

Q: How does knowing this help you with your stress levels today?

Q: What pain do you most look forward to leaving behind?

Annie said, "A lot of my friends' parents were divorcing, and they seemed to be okay with it, but I thought my world was being ripped apart."

Q: Thinking about one of your friends who has gone through their parents' divorce, how would he/she describe the experience?

Right after her parents' divorce, Annie said, "I started packing things away. Maybe I thought I would run away; maybe I just wanted to protect the things I loved the most and have them close to me all the time."

> *Have you ever felt stressed enough at home that you packed a bag to run away?*

Q: Have you ever felt stressed enough at home that you packed a bag to run away? What happened?

Q: How have you protected your heart from others hurting it? Did it work? If you were going to pack a bag with the things you needed, what would you put in there?

Annie encountered an insensitive Sunday school teacher. She said, "I tried to tell her about my little bear and how scared he was sometimes. Instead of helping me, she crammed a big Bible inside my bag. She told me if I would accept Jesus, everything would get better. But I never saw Jesus—I just got the Bible. And it made my bag heavier."

Q: If you were Annie's Sunday school teacher, what would you have done differently?

Q: Why do you think the Bible didn't help Annie at this point in her life?

 read:

"You search the Scriptures because you think they give you eternal life. But the Scriptures point to me! Yet you refuse to come to me to receive this life."

(John 5:39–40, NLT)

The Pharisees (religious leaders of the day) searched through the Bible. They memorized parts of it. And yet before them stood the Author of the Bible and they missed Him!

Pray. ←

I serve a God who . . .

Split up into pairs. Each person should share one thing God has done in the past year to take/relieve a burden. How has He shouldered your pain?

The Pharisees (religious leaders of the day) searched through the Bible. They memorized parts of it. And yet before them stood the Author of the Bible and they missed Him!

Instead of praying, say these words as a group: "I serve a God who. . . ." Then each person says what God did in their partner's life.

For example, if Georgia shared that God helped her stop stressing over homework, her partner Shara would say, "I serve a God who helps us deal with stress."

A Better Answer

BY TODD M. CLEMENTS, M.D.

In recent years suicide increased to become the third leading cause of death among adolescents.[1]

It is nothing short of a tragedy for teenagers with so many of life's great joys ahead (living on their own, perhaps getting married, having kids, traveling the world) to cut it short by their own hand. Worst of all, suicide is a permanent solution to temporary problems, the kind that can often be solved with help that is readily available. But many teenagers feel despair over problems they never talk about, and a better answer than suicide never gets considered.

Sadly, teenagers who attempt suicide have given in to faulty thinking. They wrongly believe that how they feel will never change. Their circumstances are forever and nothing will ever be any different. Which is simply not true.

A few other things that many teenagers are unaware of about suicidal thoughts:

- Being under the influence of drugs and alcohol leads you to act in ways that you normally wouldn't—especially when it comes to doing things impulsively. Suicide is often an impulsive behavior.
- Psychological problems, like depression and anxiety, can cause suicidal thoughts. These conditions can be treated, and the dark thoughts can go away.
- False suicide attempts (when someone doesn't really intend to kill himself/herself) can accidentally be fatal or cause irreparable harm.
- Others will miss you if you die, but they will move on with life.
- Having someone to talk to when you feel suicidal is very helpful—this is why suicide hotlines are successful.

If you've had suicidal thoughts I urge you to find someone safe you can call when those feelings come again. Make that plan now, before those feelings come, so you know what to do.

One more thing you must know: Without exception, every teenage patient I've had who attempted suicide but lived, said they are very glad that they didn't die. The smarter teenager learns the better answer to suicidal thoughts is to change their life instead of taking it.

Dr. Todd Clements *is a board-certified psychiatrist and is the medical director of the Clements Clinic in Plano, Texas.*

---

1   Centers for Disease Control and Prevention, National Center for Injury Prevention and Control. Web-based Injury Statistics Query and Reporting System (WISQARS), http://www.cdc.gov/injury/wisqars/index.html/.

create.

Annie carried a lot:

1. Her parents' divorce
2. Her own expectations of perfection
3. Her parents' vying for her approval
4. Having to act like a parent
5. Her relationship with a boy that ended badly
6. Her desire to be a certain weight, look a certain way
7. A job
8. School stress
9. Church stress
10. Her friend's suicide

What do you carry?

Activity: Write 'em down, give 'em away.

Grab a piece of plain white paper and fold it in half vertically. On the left-hand side, list the things you carried five years ago. On the right-hand side, list what you carry now. Homework? Friends? Conflict with your parents? Dating? Church? Sports? Activities? Hanging out?

Take it further:

Take out a fresh piece of paper. Cut out pictures from magazines and create a collage of what you carry today, then paste it to the paper. Use this as an artistic reminder to pray that Jesus would take and carry your burdens.

deep.

on your own study #2.

Consider, Lord, how your servants are disgraced! I carry in my heart the insults of so many people.

(Psalm 89:50, NLT)

We all carry those words, don't we? The words spoken over us that we wished never had breath.

Annie felt this, no doubt, when her boyfriend walked away. She said, "He was really cute, and I guess you could say we 'fell' for each other. I thought the best way I could show him how I felt was to open my bag for him. I tried to tell him about the things that I loved and how I was afraid that I would lose them if I didn't carry them with me. He acted like he was interested and that he cared about the things I cared about. He took some of the things I gave him, then he decided he didn't like me anymore. And they were trashed. I didn't want to open my suitcase ever again. I guess I still had my things, but they were different somehow."

Q: When have you opened the bag of your heart, only to have someone reject you? How did you feel?

There's a fine line between entrusting yourself to people and guarding your heart. It's a lifelong lesson, learning to open up yet being careful about who you trust.

When have you opened the bag of your heart, only to have someone reject you? How did you feel?

read:

Above all else, guard your heart, for it is the wellspring of life.

(Proverbs 4:23, NIV)

Sometimes we're so empty, we give our hearts to anyone we think might fill them.

Q: Have you done that? What happened?

Q: Can one person fill a heart? Should they?

Q: What is one way you can guard your heart this week?

While some may want to leave us or speak awful words to us, others put pressure on us.

Annie said, "I tried to concentrate on my schoolwork, but I couldn't. My bags were getting so heavy. I had teachers that put a lot of pressure on me. They kept telling me how smart I was, and how if I would study more and work harder my grades would be better and I could get into a really good college, which I really wanted to do. I know that they couldn't see all that I was already carrying so they loaded me up with all the books I would need to learn what I needed to know."

Q: Who in your life (if any) puts pressure on you about grades?

Q: What about you? Do you stress yourself out over getting the right class rank? Why? Do others around you stress how important grades are?

Q: When you achieve something, how long does the feeling of accomplishment last? Do you take a moment to celebrate, or do you move on to the next goal?

read:

Better one handful with tranquility than two handfuls with toil and chasing after the wind.
(Ecclesiastes 4:6, NIV)

Q: What would a tranquil life look like for you today?

Annie worried about how she looked. She said, "I started obsessing about how heavy I felt. Every single day I felt bigger than all the other girls around me. I thought I didn't have enough friends because I had so many bags. I wondered if I ate less and worked out more if I could shed some of this weight. So I started running on the treadmill and eating just carrots, but I couldn't make it better. I think I lost weight, but with all these bags, I just couldn't work out so good."

> *"Better one handful with tranquility than two handfuls with toil and chasing after the wind."*
> ECCLESIASTES 4:6, NIV

Q: Have you ever overexercised or undereaten to lose weight? What happened?

Q: Can you really see a point where you'll be happy with how you look? What would it take to get you there?

Q: What do you think it looks like to be truly content with how you look? Have you ever known anyone who is content with how he/she looks?

Q: In our thin-crazy, extremely fit society, do you think it's an impossible dream to be happy with who you are? Why or why not?

The apostle Paul learned to be content in everything—a very hard lesson to learn. He wrote, "I am not saying this because I am in need, for I have learned to be content whatever the circumstances. I know what it is to be in need, and I know what it is to have plenty. I have learned the secret of being content in any and every situation, whether well fed or hungry, whether living in plenty or in want" (Philippians 4:11–12, NIV).

Q: Looking back over this lesson, how have you found contentment after someone's rejection? When you've failed in reaching a goal? When you look in the mirror?

Q: What advice would you give Annie in all three of these areas?

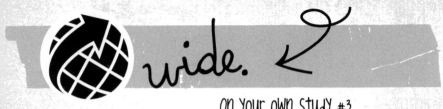

wide.

Annie is not the only one with baggage. Neither are you. We all struggle through life.

She experienced someone else's pain when she said, "There was this one guy in my math class. We talked sometimes. One day he put a gun to his head. A bunch of us attended the service and all I could think about was that he probably had a lot of bags like me and he just wanted to blow them away."

Q: What friends of yours right now are struggling? In what ways?

Q: How have you tried to help? Has it helped?

Even the apostle Paul experienced deep discouragement to the point that he despaired.

 read:

Praise be to the God and Father of our Lord Jesus Christ, the Father of compassion and the God of all comfort, who comforts us in all our troubles, so that we can comfort those in any trouble with the comfort we ourselves have received from God. For just as the sufferings of Christ flow over into our lives, so also through Christ our comfort overflows. If we are distressed, it is for your comfort and salvation; if we are comforted, it is for your comfort, which produces in you patient endurance of the same sufferings we suffer. And our hope for you is firm, because we know that just as you share in our sufferings, so also you share in our comfort.

We do not want you to be uninformed, brothers, about the hardships we suffered in the province of Asia. We were under great pressure, far beyond our ability to endure, so that we despaired even of life. Indeed, in our hearts we felt the sentence of death. But this happened that we might not rely on ourselves but on God, who raises the dead. He has delivered us from such a deadly peril, and he will deliver us. On him we have set our hope that he will continue to deliver us, as you help us by your prayers. Then many will give thanks on our behalf for the gracious favor granted us in answer to the prayers of many.

(2 Corinthians 1:3–11, NIV)

Let's look at the first part of this passage.

Q: In how many troubles does God bring comfort?

Q: Do you have to experience the same trouble to be able to comfort someone? (Note the words *all* and *any* in the beginning of the passage.

This scripture seems to give reason for our own personal pain and baggage. Once we hurt, we receive God's comfort. That comfort is so amazing, we can't help spilling it out to others who are hurting.

Q: Describe a time when God comforted you, then you turned around and offered comfort.

Now let's focus on the latter half of these verses.

Q: When have you felt overwhelmed? Burdened beyond belief? What happened?

Q: What lesson did Paul learn from his ordeal?

Q: How have you learned to lean on Jesus when things get really, really hard?

Q: When have you sensed someone's prayer for you? What happened?

Q: When have you recently prayed for someone who was going through a rough patch? How did you let him/her know you were praying?

"We were under great pressure, far beyond our ability to endure. . . . But this happened that we might not rely on ourselves but on God, who raises the dead."
2 CORINTHIANS 1:8B–9B, NIV

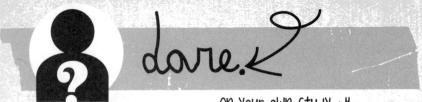

dare.

Activity: Life inventory.

The "dare" element of this inventory rests in the word *authenticity*. Answer the following questions honestly.

1. Whose expectations stress you out the most? Yours? Your parents'? Your teachers'? Your coaches'? Your friends'? God's?
2. Look back on your collage. What do you carry?
3. What is the hardest thing to let go of and give to Jesus? Why?
4. When one person disappoints you, do you tend to get over it and trust again, or do you lose faith in everyone?
5. What do you depend on in your life to get you through each day?
6. Is it hard for you to let go of control of your life and give it to Jesus? Why or why not?
7. How can Christianity be an additional weight?
8. What three things/people are truly the most important to you?
9. Who have you had to forgive recently? How hard was it to forgive?
10. Who are you still angry with? Why? What happened?
11. What distracts you from following Jesus?
12. How do you postpone dealing with something? With an activity? By just not thinking about it?
13. Is it hard for you to fit in at church? Why or why not?
14. If you're still holding on to stress and baggage, what do you gain by doing that? Why is it hard to let go?
15. Even if you've never experienced divorce, in what ways did you relate to Annie's feelings about her parents?
16. Have you ever had to be the adult in your home? When? How did that make you feel?
17. What things can you do to cope with your own baggage other than suicide or doing destructive things?
18. What does it mean to follow Jesus today for you?
19. Do you consider yourself too busy? Why or why not?
20. What one thing would you change about school?
21. When does life feel like too much?
22. Who is a person in your life who helps you carry your baggage? What does he/she do to help you?
23. If you could ask Jesus just one thing about your life today, what would it be?

Resources & iTunes List

Resources.

- *Jesus Calling*, by Sarah Young
- *Beautiful*, by Cindy Martinusen-Coloma
- *To Save a Life*, by Jim Britts and Rachel Britts
- *Shells* (Nooma video), http://www.nooma.com

 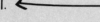

Listen. ←—————————————

- "Swallowed in the Sea" by Coldplay, *X&Y*
- "Resurrection" by Nicol Sponberg, *Resurrection*
- "Stuck in a Moment" by U2, *All That You Can't Leave Behind*